Baby Steps:
A Guide to
Maternity Leave and
Maternity Pay

Leah Stephanie Waller
Solicitor
Lennons Solicitors

D1446546

Law Brief Publishing

Published 2016 by
Law Brief Publishing
30 The Parks
Minehead
Somerset
TA24 8BT

www.lawbriefpublishing.com

Paperback: 978-1-911035-05-3
Ebook: 978-1-911035-06-0

Thank You To...

My Family

Jemma Matthews, Antonio Plaku,
Karen Waller, Nathan Waller and Stuart Waller.

My Friends

Ruth 'Phoebe' Garland, Kirstie-Lee Matthews, Rachael Owen
Kelly Startin, Lauren Turner and Coral Willingale.

With Special Thanks to...

Lennons Solicitors
Chess Chambers,
2 Broadway Court,
Chesham,
Buckinghamshire,
HP5 1EG
www.lennonssolicitors.co.uk

Contents

INTRODUCTION

In this book I will be giving a practical guide to Maternity Leave, your rights during Maternity Leave and looking at Statutory Maternity Pay for employees. I will also briefly look at Shared Parental Leave on a whistle-stop tour of an alternative option available to you.

I am not a mother myself and so will be looking from a legal perspective, as a qualified solicitor, and this guide will set out the minimum legal requirements. Please bear in mind that your employer may give better rights than these, so you should always check your contract or ask the human resources department.

As always; you know what is best and so what works for some may not work for others. Remember that these are the minimum requirements, in most circumstances, and so not an absolute rule.

The 'expected week of childbirth', often referred to as EWC in much literature, is a very important date and working this out and having this in mind throughout will be useful.

Where a 'week' is referred to, within this book, the 'week' runs from Sunday to Saturday and so the expected week of childbirth will begin on a Sunday.

Other important dates for you to be mindful of are:-

- the **Qualifying Week**; *this is the 15th week before the expected week of childbirth;*

- the date you want your **Maternity Leave** to commence;

- the date on which your **Maternity Leave will end**; *this is based on you taking the full 52 weeks or Ordinary and Additional Maternity Leave. Your employer will inform you of this.*

Maternity Leave

You have found out you are expecting... What now?

a timeline of events from when you find out you are expecting to returning to work.

Telling your employer

The latest time you can tell your employer is in the 15th week before your baby is due.
Inform your employer:
- you are pregnant
- expected week of childbirth
- date on which you intend to start your maternity leave

Ordinary Maternity Leave

First 26 weeks.
The earliest this can start is 11 weeks before the baby is due.

CONGRATULATIONS

You are now a parent to a new bundle of joy!

Additional Maternity Leave

26 weeks after Ordinary Maternity Leave.

Notice to Return

If you want to return to work before the end of your maternity leave, you must give your employer at least 8 weeks' notice of the date you will be returning.

Resign

If you are not going to return to work you must give notice in accordance with your Contract of Employment.

Return to work

52 weeks have passed since your maternity leave began and so it is now time to return to work if you have not agreed otherwise.

WHO GETS MATERNITY LEAVE?

All women employees are entitled to Ordinary Maternity Leave and Additional Maternity Leave from day one of their employment. It does not matter how many hours you work or how long you have worked for your employer. Everyone is entitled to 52 weeks of Maternity Leave, whether you were pregnant before starting the job or started the job before becoming pregnant.

Length of time with current employer	Ordinary and Additional Maternity Leave	Statutory Maternity Pay (SMP)	Time off for antenatal care	Health & Safety protection	Protection from unfair dismissal & treatment
Already pregnant when started	Yes	No, but you may qualify for Maternity Allowance	Yes	Yes	Yes
Started job before becoming pregnant and, on average, earn less than £112 per week	Yes	No, but you may qualify for Maternity Allowance	Yes	Yes	Yes
Started job before becoming pregnant and, on average, earn more than £112 per week	Yes	Yes, if eligible, if not, you may qualify for Maternity Allowance	Yes	Yes	Yes

GIVING NOTICE OF
YOUR PREGNANCY

After the joy of finding out you are pregnant comes the, often daunting, task of telling your employer the news. This will be more difficult for some than others and will often illicit different reactions depending on your working relationships, the time at which you announce your pregnancy, whether this is your first pregnancy and the structure of the organisation at the time of telling your employer.

Regardless of how difficult the issue may be, the latest time that you can tell your employer that you are pregnant is the 15th week before your baby is due.

However, you may wish to tell your employer earlier as it may be to your advantage. The advantages of telling your employer of your pregnancy at an earlier stage include:-

- Health and Safety rights during pregnancy and also whilst breastfeeding;

- the right to paid time off for antenatal care;

- legal protection from being dismissed or discriminated against on the grounds of pregnancy;

- your absence record being unaffected by any pregnancy-related illnesses.

Health and Safety during pregnancy and breastfeeding

Your employer must act in accordance with The Management of Health and Safety at Work Regulations 1999 and assess the workplace risks to any employee who is pregnant, who has given birth within the previous six months or who is breastfeeding. Following that assessment, your working conditions or working hours must, if necessary, be altered to avoid any significant risk. If it is not reasonable to alter your working hours or conditions or such alterations would not avoid the identified risks then you must be offered suitable alternative work. That alternative work must be of a kind that is suitable and appropriate for you in the circumstances and the terms and conditions of the proposed work cannot be substantially less favourable to your current terms and conditions[1]. Alternatively, your employer can suspend you on full pay[2] for as long as is necessary to avoid any identified risks.

Some of the risks identified by the Health and Safety Executive (HSE) include physical risks such as: movements and postures; manual handling; vibrations; noise and radiation; biological risks from infectious diseases and exposure to chemicals such as: toxic chemicals; mercury; pesticides; lead and carbon monoxide. Working conditions should also be considered when carrying out a risk assessment and specific risks highlighted by the HSE include: facilities at work; fatigue; working hours; stress; temperature; working at heights; travelling; personal protective equipment and

---

1 Section 67 Employment Rights Act 1996

2 Section 68 Employment Rights Act 1996

working with Visual Display Units. Evidently not all of these risks will apply to every job and some jobs will pose more risks than others to expectant mothers. Each risk assessment is carried out by your employer on a case by case basis.

Working nights whilst pregnant

If you work night shifts, there is nothing to prevent you from continuing to do so whilst you are pregnant unless your midwife or GP provides you with a medical certificate stating that you cannot work night shifts.

If you do have a certificate from your midwife or GP then your employer may offer you suitable alternative work during the day, on the same terms as your usual night shift employment, and this will include being paid at the same rate of pay that you would have been paid had you continued working night shifts. However, if there is no suitable altern-ative work that your employer can offer you then you must be suspended from work on full pay for as long as is necessary to avoid the identified risk of working at night.

Paid time off for antenatal care

Your employer must give you reasonable paid time off for antenatal care[3] once they are aware that you are pregnant. Your employer cannot ask you to make this time up, if taken in your usual working hours, or ask you to use your annual

---

3 Section 56 Employment Rights Act 1996

leave. You should be paid your usual rate of pay for any time that you take off in relation to antenatal care.

The antenatal care must be an appointment, that has been arranged as a result of medical advice received from a registered medical practitioner, registered midwife or registered nurse[4] and can include medical examinations, scans, antenatal classes and parenting or relaxation classes.

Your employer may ask you to provide a copy of your Maternity Certificate and an appointment card, or similar, evidencing your antenatal care appointment and you should comply with this request.

Your spouse, civil partner, the expectant father of the child, or your partner is also entitled to unpaid time off to attend two antenatal appointments, with each appointment being a maximum of six and a half hours[5]. Again, the appointment must have been arranged because of medical advice received from a registered medical practitioner, registered midwife or registered nurse. In order to take this time off they will need to advise their employer of their relationship with you or the expected child and that the antenatal appointment has been arranged on the advice of a registered medical practitioner, registered midwife or registered nurse as well as the date and time of the appointment[6]. They may be asked to provide a

---

4 Section 55 Employment Rights Act 1996

5 Section 57ZE Employment Rights Act 1996

6 Section 57ZE Employment Rights Act 1996

copy of your Maternity Certificate and an appointment card, or similar, evidencing the antenatal care appointment.

Pregnancy-related illness

If you are absent from work due to a pregnancy-related illness, then this should be dealt with differently to a 'normal' sickness absence and should be recorded separately as it will not count towards your sickness record.

This is important in the case of a redundancy situation arising as absence records may be taken into consideration when making redundancy selections and any time off that you have had in relation to your pregnancy will not be included if absence records are a criterion that is looked at when selecting employees for redundancy.

You will receive sick pay in the usual way if you are absent from work for a pregnancy-related illness, and this will be as set out in your Contract of Employment, whether that is Statutory Sick Pay or an enhanced sick pay offered under your Contract of Employment.

If you are absent from work due to a pregnancy-related illness in the final four weeks prior to the expected week of childbirth and you have not yet begun your Maternity Leave then your Maternity Leave will automatically start on the day after your first day of absence in that four-week period.

What should you tell your employer?

It is important to inform your employer that you are pregnant as, in order to be eligible for Maternity Leave, you must give your employer the following information in or before the 15th week before expected childbirth (if requested, this information must be put it in writing):-

- That you are pregnant; *your employer may request a copy of a certificate from a registered medical practitioner or midwife and a copy of your Maternity Certificate is sufficient.*

- The expected week of childbirth.

- The date on which you intend to start your maternity leave[7].

Although your employer may not request written notification, it is advisable to give written notification as the employer's Health and Safety obligations are not activated until they receive notification of your pregnancy in writing.

If you are unable to inform your employer of your pregnancy in, or before, the Qualifying Week (the 15th week before expected childbirth) because it was not reasonably practicable for you to do so then your failure will be overlooked and you must inform your employer as soon as you are able to.

---

7   Regulation 4 The Maternity and Parental Leave etc. Regulations 1999

If you are not aware of your pregnancy until after the 15th week of expected childbirth or you start work with your employer after the 15th week of expected childbirth, then it will not be considered reasonably practicable for you to have advised your employer in or before the Qualifying Week and your failure will be overlooked.

Changing the date that your Maternity Leave begins

If you want to change the date that you start your Maternity Leave after you have given notice to your employer, then the date on which you will have to advise your employer will depend on whether you want to bring your Maternity Leave closer or move it to a later date.

If you want to start your Maternity Leave sooner, then you must give at least 28 days' notice to your employer prior to the new intended start date. If you wish to put your Maternity Leave back to a later date, then you must give your employer notice 28 days' prior to the original intended start date. If there is a good reason why that is not possible, you must tell your employer as soon as you reasonably can.

Employer's response

Once you have given notice to your employer of your pregnancy your employer must write to you, within 28 days of that notice, and state the date that you are expected to return from Maternity Leave (52 weeks after the start date of your Maternity Leave).

If you vary the start date of your Maternity Leave then your employer will have to write to you again, within 28 days of that notification of variation, setting out the new date that you are expected to return to work following your Maternity Leave.

BEFORE GOING ON MATERNITY LEAVE

Before you leave work to go on Maternity Leave it is advisable to have a meeting with your employer to discuss what is going to happen during your Maternity Leave, who will be covering your work and how your return to work will be dealt with. This will also give you the opportunity to raise any issues or questions that you may have.

Some issues that could be dealt with during this meeting include:-

- who will be dealing with your work whilst you are away and any hand over period;

- when your Statutory Maternity Pay will start and how much you will receive;

- how you would like to be contacted, and how often you would like to be contacted, during your Maternity Leave (email, phone, text message, post);

- the possibility of Keeping in Touch Days;

- the possibility of flexible working and the procedure for requesting this (although you may wish to wait until after your baby is born and you have a childcare plan in place to raise this).

MATERNITY LEAVE

Maternity Leave is for a maximum of 52 weeks. The earliest that Maternity Leave can start is the 11th week before expected childbirth[1] and this leave is split into two periods: -

- Ordinary Maternity Leave
  This is the first 26 weeks of your Maternity Leave.

- Additional Maternity Leave
  This is a maximum of 26 weeks following Ordinary Maternity Leave.

You are entitled to Ordinary Maternity Leave and Additional Maternity Leave from day one of your employment regardless of how many hours you work or how long you have worked for your employer, whether you were pregnant before starting the job or started the job before becoming pregnant.

You are entitled to Maternity Leave regardless of how early your baby is born and you are also entitled to Maternity Leave if your baby dies after the birth or is stillborn after the end of the 24th week of pregnancy.

---

1   Regulation 4 The Maternity and Parental Leave etc. Regulations 1999

Maternity Leave that starts automatically

If you are off work due to a pregnancy-related illness in the final four weeks prior to the expected week of childbirth and you have not yet begun your Maternity Leave then your Maternity Leave will automatically start on the day after your first day of absence in that four-week period (the second consecutive day that you are absent from work). However, if you are absent for illness unrelated to your pregnancy this will not trigger the automatic commencement of Maternity Leave.

If your baby arrives early, and prior to commencing Maternity Leave, then your Maternity Leave will begin on the day after childbirth.

In both of these situations, if you are ill with a pregnancy-related illness in the four weeks prior to the expected week of childbirth or if you give birth before your Maternity Leave begins, then you must notify your employer that you are absent from work due to your pregnancy and the employer's obligation to provide you with notice of your date of return will kick in and a new notification should be issued to you by your employer stating the new date on which you are expected to return to work.

Ordinary Maternity Leave

Ordinary Maternity Leave is the first 26 weeks of your Maternity Leave[2] and so will include the time that you are on leave prior to the birth of your child, depending on when you decide to take Maternity Leave from.

Maternity Leave can be taken any time from the 11th week prior to the expected week of childbirth but when you take your leave is a matter for you to decide. Many mothers decide to work as close to their due date as possible to increase their time with their child after the birth before returning to work.

If you return to work after your Ordinary Maternity Leave, after 26 weeks of Maternity Leave, without taking your Additional Maternity Leave entitlement then you have the right to return to the same job that you were doing prior to your Maternity Leave[3] as long as you have given your employer the correct notice in order to qualify for Maternity Leave (as set out previously).

In legal terms; if you return to work after your Ordinary Maternity Leave then you must be offered the same job in terms of its nature (as set out in your Contract of Employment), capacity (in terms of the position of authority) and at the same place of work.

---

2 Section 71 Employment Rights Act 1996

3 Regulation 18(1) The Maternity and Parental Leave etc. Regulations 1999

Additional Maternity Leave

It is up to you whether you take Additional Maternity Leave, this is the 26 weeks following Ordinary Maternity Leave, and you may decide to take none, some or all of this time before returning to work.

If you return to work after, or during, your Additional Maternity Leave then you have the right to return to the same job but, if this is not reasonably practicable, your employer can offer a suitable and appropriate alternative job on similar terms and conditions[4]. Again, the terms of any alternative position will be considered, specifically in terms of its nature (as set out in your Contract of Employment), capacity (in terms of the position of authority) and the intended place of work. The alternative role must be as close as possible to your previous role with the employer before your Maternity Leave commenced.

If you are offered an alternative role, then the level of seniority must be the same as that of your previous role and you will be entitled to the same pension rights. You will also be entitled to benefit from similar rights to those that you were entitled to in your previous role and suffer no less favourable terms.

If the role is less senior or you have less responsibility or less interesting work to do in the proposed alternative role, then it

---

4   Regulation 18(2) The Maternity and Parental Leave etc. Regulations 1999

is unlikely that this proposed role will satisfy the test of being a suitable alternative with no less favourable terms.

The burden of proof is on your employer to demonstrate that it is not reasonably practicable for you to return to your previous role.

If a member of temporary staff is brought in to cover your work during your Maternity Leave and your employer prefers their style of working; it will not be deemed as reasonably practicable to offer you an alternative role rather than your previous role, in order for your temporary replacement to take over your previous role on a full-time basis, you must be able to return to your previous role.

RIGHTS DURING
MATERNITY LEAVE

During your Maternity Leave, both Ordinary and Additional, your statutory rights continue as do your contractual rights.

Your statutory rights include:-

- 28 days paid annual leave (including bank holidays);

  You may be entitled to more under your Contract of Employment so it is worth checking this as your holiday entitlement continues to accrue whilst you are on Maternity Leave and your holiday cannot be taken during your Maternity Leave so you will be able to take this following your return to work.

- Protection against discrimination by failing to consider you for opportunities such as promotion or a pay rise;

- Protection against unfair dismissal and unfair treatment or discrimination.

Your contractual rights are the benefits that you are entitled to under your Contract of Employment and these may be more favourable than the statutory rights.

Whilst you are on Maternity Leave your Contract of Employment continues as though you are still working and you are entitled to benefit from all the terms under your

Contract as though you are not on leave except for the benefit of remuneration[1]. You also remain bound by any terms of your Contract, such as restrictive covenants, although you will not be expected to attend your place of work, carry out your job role or the stipulated working hours under your Contract whilst on Maternity Leave. Any Disciplinary and Grievance procedures or policies that your employer has in place will also continue to apply throughout your Maternity Leave.

The contractual rights that continue during your Maternity Leave will be different in each individual's Contract but may include private health insurance, dental care, share schemes, pension contributions, gym membership and annual leave (over and above the Statutory entitlement). If you are unable to use your holiday entitlement within your employer's holiday year, because you are on Maternity Leave, then you are permitted to carry this over even if the company's usual holiday policy does not allow for accrued but untaken holidays to be carried over.

If you are permitted the use of a company car, car allowance, mobile phone and laptop for personal use as well as business use then this entitlement will also continue throughout your Maternity Leave, if however, the use of any of these benefits is for business use only then this contractual entitlement will not continue throughout your Maternity Leave.

---

1   Section 71 Employment Rights Act 1996

You will not be entitled to remuneration in the usual way, in accordance with your Contract of Employment, throughout your Maternity Leave and so any wages, salary or payment that is related to your performance, such as performance-related bonuses or commission, will not be payable during your Maternity Leave. You will, of course, be entitled to any performance-related bonus or commission payments that you earnt prior to your Maternity Leave, as well as an additional two weeks' of performance-related bonus or commission payments, to take into account the Compulsory Maternity Leave period.

If any bonuses are given, by your employer, whilst you are on Maternity Leave that are not performance related and are given to all staff then you should receive this in full as though you are not absent from work.

Reasonable Contact

During your Maternity Leave your employer is allowed to make "Reasonable contact from time to time"[2] with you and what is considered reasonable will very much depend on the circumstances of each individual.

Reasonable contact from your employer may include giving you information, or contacting you, in relation to:-

- arranging Keeping in Touch Days;

- arranging your return to work;

- advising you of any changes or developments at work;

- social events or team building events;

- training courses and events;

- advising you of colleagues who are leaving;

- new staff;

You should be kept informed, under all circumstances, of any promotion opportunities or vacancies that arise whilst you are on Maternity Leave.

2   Regulation 12A(4) The Maternity and Parental Leave etc Regulations 1999

Keeping in Touch Days

During your Maternity Leave you are entitled to have up to ten Keeping in Touch Days (KiT Days) and this will not have any impact on your Maternity Leave rights[3].

Your KiT Days should be arranged with your employer and must be an agreement between both you and your employer but there is no obligation on your employer to offer KiT Days and neither is there any obligation on you to work any KiT Days. However, these KiT Days are useful for managing your return to work.

KiT Days can be used for carrying out your usual job role but can also be used for training, conferences, team meetings or attending events. However, it is worth noting that any work carried out on a day, or part of a day, during your Maternity Leave will be classed as a day's work and so even if you only attend a 30-minute team meeting or a half-day conference these will both use one KiT Day each.

You are entitled to payment for your work during a KiT Day and the amount you are paid should be agreed with your employer.

You cannot work any KiT Days within the Compulsory Maternity Leave period (the first two weeks after childbirth).

---

3 Regulation 12A(1) The Maternity and Parental Leave etc Regulations 1999

HOW MUCH MATERNITY LEAVE SHOULD I TAKE?

It is ultimately up to you how much Maternity Leave you take and this may depend on arrangements in place following your return to work, the type of work that you do and your childcare arrangements.

Whether you intend to return to work after your Maternity Leave or not; you do not need to inform your employer of how long you will be taking for Maternity Leave. Your employer should assume that you will be taking 52 weeks of Maternity Leave and when they give you notice of your return to work date it will be presumed that the full 52 weeks of Ordinary and Additional Maternity Leave will be taken.

By law, you are not able to work for the first two weeks after childbirth, or four weeks if you work in a factory, and this initial period is known as Compulsory Maternity Leave[1].

If you decide not to take all of your Maternity Leave and return to work prior to the end of your Additional Maternity Leave, then you must give eight weeks' notice to your employer in order return to work early. (*This is dealt with in more detail later on*).

---

1 Section 72 Employment Rights Act 1996 and Regulation 8 The Maternity and Parental Leave etc. Regulations 1999

SHARED PARENTAL LEAVE

Although it is not my intention to deal with the subject of Shared Parental Leave in any great detail within this book; it is important to mention Shared Parental Leave so that you are aware of this as another consideration when making arrangements for your return to work.

Shared Parental Leave enables you to share 50 weeks of your Maternity Leave (remembering that the first two weeks after your baby has been born is Compulsory Maternity Leave) with your partner if both of you qualify for Shared Parental Leave.

If you return to work before the end of your full Maternity Leave you can share any remaining Maternity Leave with your partner as Shared Parental Leave. Shared Parental Leave can be taken at the same time as your partner or at different times.

Shared Parental Leave must take place within one year of your baby's birth and is for a maximum of 50 weeks to be shared between both you and your partner. Up to 37 of those 50 weeks can be paid and this Pay is at the same rate as Statutory Maternity Pay.

By way of example;

if you take only your Ordinary Maternity Leave and return to work after 26 weeks of Maternity Leave, you will have 13 weeks of Shared Parental Leave, as will your partner (the remaining 26 weeks of Maternity Leave divided between two of you) to take within one year of your baby's birth and this can be taken at the same time as your partner or at a separate time.

As with Maternity Leave; the rules in relation to eligibility for Shared Parental Leave apply and the correct notices need to be given to your employer in order to take the entitlement.

DISMISSAL AND REDUNDANCY DURING MATERNITY LEAVE

This chapter sets out a brief outline of the legal claims that may arise if you are dismissed or if you are made redundant during your pregnancy or whilst on Maternity Leave but it is advisable to take legal advice on your individual situation should this arise.

Unfair Dismissal

If you are not able to return to work following your Maternity Leave, whether in your previous role or a suitable alternative role, then you will be deemed to be unfairly dismissed unless your employer can justify their reasons for not allowing you to return to your previous role or a suitable alternative role.

If there is a suitable vacancy and this is not offered to you, following your return from Maternity Leave, then your dismissal will automatically be unfair.

An unfair dismissal may also give rise to a claim for discrimination in relation to your sex.

Set out below is a non-exhaustive list of circumstances in which you will also be deemed to be unfairly dismissed if the only, or principal, reason for your dismissal is due to any of the following[1]:-

---

1 Regulation 20 The Maternity and Parental Leave etc. Regulations 1999

- your pregnancy;

- that you have given birth to a child;

- that you took or intended to take Ordinary Maternity Leave;

- that you took or intended to take Additional Maternity Leave;

Constructive Dismissal

If you return to work, or intend to return to work, but your employer has made a material change to your Contract of Employment then you may be entitled to leave your employment and issue a claim for Constructive Dismissal.

Redundancy

If a genuine redundancy situation arises whilst you are on Maternity Leave your employer must offer you any suitable alternative work that is available and offer to you any appropriate vacancies. This offer of suitable vacancies must be given to you first above any other employees that have also been selected for redundancy.

When making a selection for redundancy you will be treated equally to all other employees and should not receive any favourable treatment in the selection process. However, if attendance is a criterion that is considered by your employer, within the redundancy selection process, then any absence that you have had as a result of your pregnancy or pregnancy-related illnesses will not be taken into consideration.

When offering you suitable alternative employment, where a redundancy situation has arisen, the new contract that you are offered must be for work that is suitable and appropriate, so any increase in travelling or childcare costs may be taken into consideration, and the alternative role must be on terms that are no less favourable in relation to your authority, place of work and other imposed terms and conditions.

If there is a genuine redundancy situation and there are no suitable vacancies, then your employer may make you redundant. If this occurs then you will be entitled to the notice pay, in accordance with your Contract of Employment or Statutory Notice Pay if your Contract is silent on this, and Redundancy Pay, again as provided for in your Contract of Employment or Statutory Redundancy Payment if your Contract is silent in relation to this.

Any Redundancy Payment will be calculated as though you are still at work and not on Maternity Leave as the calculation is based on your weekly pay and this is likely to put you at a significant disadvantage if your weekly pay during Maternity Leave is used for the calculation as opposed to your weekly pay had you been working your usual hours under your usual Contract of Employment.

If you are made redundant whilst on Maternity Leave then it may give rise to a claim for pregnancy and maternity discrimination if there is not a genuine redundancy situation, or if there is a genuine redundancy situation but your Maternity Leave was taken into account when making the selection for redundancies, or if you were not consulted properly because you were on Maternity Leave.

Notice Period

If either you or your employer wants to terminate the Contract of Employment, then the notice period in your Contract will still apply during your Maternity Leave.

If your Contract of Employment is silent in relation to notice periods, then the Statutory Notice Period[2] will apply and so your employer should give you one week's notice if you have been employed for longer than one month but for less than two years or one week's notice for each year you have worked, if you have worked there for two years or more. If you have been employed by the employer for twelve years or more then you are entitled to twelve weeks' notice. If you wish to give your employer notice, then you will be required to give one week's notice unless your Contract of Employment states otherwise.

---

2 Section 86 Employment Rights Act 1996

RETURNING TO WORK

If you are going to return to work after taking the full 52 weeks of Ordinary and Additional Maternity Leave then you do not need to give any notice of return, you simply go to work on the day that you are due back as stated in the notice that your employer gave to you after you informed them of your pregnancy.

If you cannot return to work on the date that your employer is expecting you to return then you must notify your employer in the usual way as if you were working and so if you are ill then you must follow any sickness/absence policy that your employer has in place.

If you want to return to work before the end of your full 52 weeks of Maternity Leave then you must give your employer at least eight weeks' notice of the date you will be returning[1]. If you do not give your employer this notice and just turn up at work before the end of your Maternity Leave, and the date on which your employer thinks that you are returning, then your employer can postpone your start date for up to eight weeks or until the end of your leave, whichever is earlier.

If you return to work immediately after, or within, the first 26 weeks of Maternity Leave (Ordinary Maternity Leave) then you have the right to return to the same job that you were doing prior to your Maternity Leave. However, if you return to work after, or during, your Additional Maternity Leave then you have the right to return to the same job but,

---

1   Regulation 11(1) The Maternity and Parental Leave etc. Regulations 1999

if this is not reasonably practicable, your employer can offer a suitable and appropriate alternative job on similar terms and conditions.

Requesting Flexible Hours

If you want to return to work but do not feel that you can commit to returning full-time or to the hours you were previously working then you have the right to make a request to your employer for flexible working. A request for flexible working may consider a change in the hours that you work, the times that you work, or even your place of work[2].

If you do want to make a request for flexible working then this should be done in accordance with any policy that your employer has in place but in any event the request must be in writing and should state that you are making a request for flexible working, what change you are asking for and when you would like this to start. You should also include in the request how this change may impact your employer and how this could be dealt with[3].

Your request for flexible working must be dealt with by your employer within three months[4] however, making a request for flexible working does not mean that your employer will accept your request but your employer does have a duty to seriously consider your request and if your employer does not

---

2 Section 80F(1) The Employment Rights Act 1996

3 Section 80F(2) The Employment Rights Act 1996

4 Section 80F(2) The Employment Rights Act 1996

agree to your request for flexible working then they must demonstrate a good business reason for refusing your request.

Reasons for which your employer could justifiable refuse your request for flexible working include where there are additional costs involved to the business, where there will be a detrimental effect on the employer's ability to meet customer demand, where they are unable to reorganise existing staff or unable to recruit new staff, where there would be a detrimental impact on quality or performance, or where there is insufficient work to do at the days or times that you have proposed[5].

You can only make one request to your employer for flexible working every twelve months[6] and so if your request is reasonably refused you will not be able to make another request until one year after the date of your last request.

In practical terms; if you want to make a request for flexible working ready for your return after Maternity Leave, you should do this at least three months before you intend to return to work as your employer can take up to three months to respond to your request and, if your request is agreed, you will want this is place ready for your return to work.

---

5   Section 80G(1)(b) The Employment Rights Act 1996

6   Section 80G The Employment Rights Act 1996

Resigning and not returning to work

If you do not want to return to work after your Maternity Leave then you must give your employer notice in accordance with your Contract of Employment. Thus if you have to give one month's notice under your Contract of Employment you should hand your notice in to your employer at least one month prior to your Maternity Leave ending. However, it may be that you want to notify your employer earlier than is strictly necessary that you do not intend to return to work after your Maternity Leave and in some cases you may wish to hand your notice in earlier than your Contract of Employment requires but still give your last day of Maternity Leave as the date on which your employment ends in order that your Statutory Maternity Pay, accrued holiday entitlements and any other employee benefits that you receive, continue to accrue up until the end of your full Maternity Leave.

If you do not have a Contract of employment or there is nothing in your Contract in relation to how much notice must be given, then you should give one week's notice to your employer that you do not intend to return.

You will be entitled to holiday pay for the holiday entitlement that you have accrued whilst on Maternity Leave even if you do not return to work after your Maternity Leave as your holiday entitlement continues to accrue throughout your Maternity Leave and up until your notice period ends.

BREASTFEEDING

If you decide to breastfeed your baby then this may impact on when you feel you can return to work and your employer must take this into consideration in relation to both breast-feeding your child and expressing milk. As with most issues; it will be best to discuss this with your employer before you return to work, when discussing the arrangements for your return, and ensuring that both you and your employer are aware of and comfortable and satisfied with the arrangements proposed.

Your employer must assess the risk, to you, of breastfeeding your baby and expressing milk and whether there is anything that it is reasonably practicable to do to control those risks. Your employer must provide you with suitable facilities to rest and take meal breaks[1] and this should include somewhere for you to lie down. It is not suitable for your employer to advise you that their toilet facilities can be used for expressing milk.

There is no legal requirement for your employer to allow you time off of work for breastfeeding however it may be an act of discrimination if your employer fails to allow you flexibility within your working day to breastfeed or express milk.

---

1   Regulation 25(4) The Workplace (Health, Safety and Welfare) Regulations 1992

Calculating Statutory Maternity Pay

26 weeks prior to Qualifying Week

Must have commenced employment with your employer by this date to be eligible.

Pregnancy begins

8 weeks / 2 months prior to EWC

Beginning of period used for calculating SMP - Must earn an average of £112.00 per week (2016/2017)

15 weeks prior to EWC - Qualifying Week

Date you must notify your employer by.

11 weeks prior to EWC

Earliest date at which your SMP can start.

Expected Week of Childbirth (EWC)

STATUTORY MATERNITY PAY

Statutory Maternity Pay is paid for a maximum of 39 weeks and to be entitled to this Pay you must give your employer 28 days' notice of the date that you want to start receiving your Statutory Maternity Pay and a copy of your Maternity Certificate (form MAT B1) stating your Expected Week of Childbirth. Your midwife or GP will give you a copy of your Maternity Certificate when you are around 20 weeks into your pregnancy and, if you wish to do so, you can give notice of your Maternity Leave and Statutory Maternity Pay at the same time, in the 15th week before your baby is due.

Your Statutory Maternity Pay will be paid to you by your employer who will then able to claim most, or all, of this back from HM Revenue and Customs.

You will be eligible for Statutory Maternity Pay if you are an employee or an office holder and pay Class 1 National Insurance contributions and have an average weekly pay of £112.00 (2015/2016 and 2016/2017). You must also have 26 weeks' continuous employment, with your employer, up to and including the 15th week before the Expected Week of Childbirth, thus you must have commenced employment with your employer, at least 11 weeks prior to becoming pregnant, in order to be entitled to Statutory Maternity Pay.

Calculating your average weekly pay

Calculating your average weekly pay is important and necessary to assess whether you are entitled to Statutory Maternity Pay.

Your average weekly pay is calculated by taking an average of your pay in the eight weeks or two months, depending on when you receive payment from your employer, prior to the last pay day before the end of the 15th week before the Expected Week of Childbirth.

If you are paid monthly; you will calculate your weekly pay as follows:-

- use your two months of payslips received for the last two months prior to the 15th week before expected childbirth;

- add the total pay from both payslips together and divide this by two (the number of months) to get your average monthly pay;

- take the average monthly figure and multiply this by 12 to get your average annual pay;

- divide this average annual pay by 52 to calculate average weekly pay.

If you are paid weekly; you will calculate your weekly pay as follows:-

- use your eight weeks' worth of payslips received for the eight weeks prior to the 15th week before the Expected Week of Childbirth;

- add the total pay from all pay slips together to calculate your total pay over the eight-week period;

- divide the total pay you received over eight weeks by eight to calculate your average weekly pay

The amount of average weekly pay that is necessary in order to qualify for Statutory Maternity Pay, currently £112.00 in 2016/2017, is the same as the 'Lower Earnings Limit' that is required before you have to pay any National Insurance contributions and this is set each tax year by the government.

Dismissal or Resignation and Statutory Maternity Pay

If you are dismissed or you resign following the 15th week before the Expected Week of Childbirth, and so after you have advised your employer of your pregnancy and intention to receive Maternity Leave and Statutory Maternity Pay, then you will still be entitled to receive Statutory Maternity Pay. This is applicable even if you only work one day during the 15th week before the Expected Week of Childbirth.

Repaying your Statutory Maternity Pay if you do not return to work

If you do not return to work after your Maternity Leave then you do not have to repay any of the Statutory Maternity Pay that you have received. However, if you start work for another employer whilst still receiving Statutory Maternity Pay then this pay will cease as you will be employed and earning a wage.

How much is Statutory Maternity Pay?

In the first six weeks of your Maternity Leave you will receive 90% of your average pay and your average pay is calculated from the pay you actually received in the eight weeks or two months, depending on when you receive payment from your employer, up to the last pay day before the end of the 15th week before the Expected Week of Childbirth (*please see the calculations above*).

For the remainder of the 39 weeks of your Statutory Maternity Pay period, thus the remaining 33 weeks, you will be paid £139.58 per week (2016/2017), or 90% of your average earnings if that is lower. The Statutory Maternity Pay rate is reviewed in April each year.

Your employer pays your Statutory Maternity Pay in the same way as your salary is paid and so any tax and National Insurance contributions will be deducted before being paid to you.

Your Statutory Maternity Pay is not affected by working any Keeping in Touch Days unless you work for more than 10 KiT Days.

Pay rises

Your Statutory Maternity Pay is calculated using the eight-week, or two month, period prior to the 15th week before the Expected Week of Childbirth. However, if you receive a pay rise after this calculating period but whilst still on either Ordinary or Additional Maternity Leave then you will be entitled to include this higher amount of pay as though the pay rise took place at the beginning of the period used for calculating the average weekly pay[1].

If you are not aware of this pay rise until after your Statutory Maternity Pay has commenced, then your Statutory Maternity Pay will be re-calculated as and when appropriate and then any additional payments will be made to you.

When will you receive Statutory Maternity Pay?

As with Maternity Leave; the earliest you can start receiving your Statutory Maternity Pay is 11 weeks before the Expected Week of Childbirth. However, you can work right up until the date the baby is born, unless you have a pregnancy-related illness or absence in the last four weeks of your pregnancy or

---

1   Regulation 21(7) The Statutory Maternity Pay (General) Regulations 1986

your baby is born before you have started your Maternity Leave and your Maternity Leave starts automatically.

Your Statutory Maternity Pay will usually start on the same day as your Maternity Leave.

When does your Statutory Maternity Pay Stop?

You Statutory Maternity will continue for a maximum of 39 weeks unless you return to work prior to the end of this 39-week period, in which case your Statutory Maternity Leave will not be paid and you will receive your usual salary under your Contract of Employment[2].

Your Statutory Maternity Pay will end prior to the end of the 39-week period if you commence work for an alternative employer whilst still in receipt of Statutory Maternity Pay[3], if you are detained in legal custody or if you are sentenced to a term of imprisonment whilst still in receipt of Statutory Maternity Pay.[4] If you pass away during the 39-week period in which Statutory Maternity Pay is paid to you[5] your Statutory Maternity Pay will also end.

Your Statutory Maternity Pay will continue where KiT Days are worked as this does not constitute a full return to work

2 Section 165(4) The Social Security Contributions and Benefits Act

3 Section 165(6) The Social Security Contributions and Benefits Act

4 Regulation 9 The Statutory Maternity Pay (General) Regulations 1986

5 Regulation 10 The Statutory Maternity Pay (General) Regulations 1986

however any money that you do receive for your work on KiT days may be offset against your Statutory Maternity Pay.

Offsetting Statutory Maternity Pay

Any remuneration that you receive under your Contract of Employment, such as monies received for work on a KiT Day will be taken into account when paying Statutory Maternity Pay[6], unless your employer is happy to give you the benefit of time off in lieu for work completed on a KiT Day rather than pay.

> *Thus if you receive £89.58 for a day's work on a KiT Day, you would still be entitled to £139.58 in Statutory Maternity Pay for that week (£89.58 in respect of payment for your KiT Day and £50.00 in Statutory Maternity Pay).*

From a practical point of view in terms of financial benefit; it is therefore more beneficial for you, financially, to use your KiT days for the time when you are not being paid Statutory Maternity Pay as you will then receive the full pay for your KiT Days rather than this being offset against your Statutory Maternity Pay.

---

6 Regulation 19 The Statutory Maternity Pay (General) Regulations 1986 and Schedule 13 paragraph 3 The Social Security Contributions and Benefits Act

However, it may be that you and your employer can come to an agreement, such as taking time off in lieu, if both you and your employer want the KiT Days to take place during the 39-week period that you are entitled to Statutory Maternity Pay.

Maternity Allowance

If you do not qualify for Statutory Maternity Pay from your employer because you commenced employment when you were already pregnant or your earnings are below the qualifying threshold, or if you are self-employed, then your employer will complete HMRC Form SMP1 which sets out why you are not eligible to receive Statutory Maternity Pay.

Maternity Allowance is paid by your Local Jobcentre Plus for 39 weeks.

In order to qualify for Maternity Allowance; you must have been employed or self-employed for at least 26 weeks in the last 66 weeks before the Expected Week of Childbirth and have an average weekly pay of at least £30.00 over any 13-week period in the 66 weeks before the expected week of childbirth.

Other benefits

If you are not entitled to either Statutory Maternity Pay or Maternity Allowance then you may qualify for the following benefits:-

- Employment and Support Allowance (ESA)

- NI Credits

- Jobseeker's Allowance (JSA)

- Income Support

GOVERNMENT STATISTICS

The latest Government Maternity Statistics that are available, at the time of writing, are the monthly statistics for May 2016 which were published in October 2016[1]. The statistics for May 2016 were compiled from 96 NHS providers (for comparison purposes; statistics were compiled from 90 providers in March 2016 and 92 providers in April 2016) and look at the use of NHS maternity services such as booking appointments, admissions, screening tests, labour and delivery.

The statistics give a guide as to the demographic of women using NHS funded maternity services, in England, and highlighted below are some key findings:-

Antenatal Booking Appointments

- In May 2016, 40,116 women attended an NHS antenatal booking appointment (compared to 40,056 in March 2016 and 40,224 in April 2016);

- The average age of women attending NHS antenatal appointments was 30 years (up from an average of 29 in both March and April 2016);

  - 20% of women were aged 24 and under, including 4% who were under the age of 20;

  - 28% were aged 25 to 29;

---

1 Maternity Services Monthly Statistics, England – May 2016, Experimental statistics

- ○ 31% were aged 30-34; and

- ○ 21% were aged 35 and over.

Smokers

- 12% of women attending an NHS antenatal booking appointment in May 2016 were smokers;

- 77% were non-smokers; and

- 12% of women attending did not disclose, or were not asked, their smoking status.

Body Mass Index

Body Mass Index is calculated based on a person's height and weight. A score of under 20 is considered to be 'Under-weight', a score of 20 to 25 is considered 'Normal, a score of 25 to 30 is considered 'Overweight' and a score of over 30 is considered 'Obese'.

- 46% of women attending an NHS antenatal booking appointment in May 2016 were considered 'Normal';

- 8% were considered 'Underweight';

- 26% were considered 'Overweight'; and

- 20% were considered 'Obese';

Previous Caesarean Sections

- 45% of women attending an NHS antenatal booking appointment in May 2016 had not previously given birth;

- 42% of women had previously given birth but had not previously had a caesarean section; and

- 13% of women had previously had at least one caesarean section.

FREQUENTLY ASKED QUESTIONS

1. **How much Maternity Leave am I entitled to?**

    Everyone is entitled to 52 weeks of Maternity Leave.

2. **Can my employer ask me how long I will be taking for Maternity Leave or when I will return?**

    Your employer can ask you for an *indication* of when you think you will return to work and if you are thinking of requesting flexible working but you do not have to confirm how much Maternity Leave you will be taking.

    Your views may well change between embarking on Maternity Leave and giving birth to when you are arranging child care. Remember that your employer must assume that you will be taking the full 52 weeks of Maternity Leave.

3. **Does my holiday entitlement accrue whilst I am on Maternity Leave?**

    Yes; your holiday entitlement will continue to accrue whilst you are on Maternity Leave as though you were working your usual hours.

4. **Do I have to go in to work during my Maternity Leave if my employer asks me to?**

No. You are entitled to return to work for up to 10 KiT Days during your Maternity Leave, if agreed by both you and your employer, but there is no onus on you to take up the offer of KiT Days or for your employer to provide them

5. **How much contact should you have with your employer during your Maternity Leave?**

Your Employer is allowed to make *reasonable contact* from time to time with you during your Maternity Leave and this will depend on your individual circumstances. It is better to try and agree this with your employer prior to taking your Maternity Leave so that there are no surprises.

6. **If someone else is employed temporarily in my place while I am on Maternity Leave, is my job guaranteed to me when I return?**

If someone else is employed to carry out your role during your Maternity Leave this does not affect your rights when you return to work.

If you return to work immediately after, or within, the first 26 weeks of Maternity Leave (Ordinary Maternity Leave) then you have the right to return to the same job that you were doing prior to your Maternity Leave.

If you return to work after, or during, your Additional Maternity Leave then you have the right to return to the same job but, if this is not reasonably practicable, your employer can offer a suitable and appropriate alternative job on similar terms and conditions.

7. **Will my Maternity Leave be unpaid or paid?**

Whether your Maternity Leave is paid or unpaid will depend on your eligibility to receive Statutory Maternity Pay and whether your Contract of Employment includes any enhanced Maternity Pay policies.

If you are eligible for Statutory Maternity Pay; then you will be paid for a maximum of 39 weeks.

8. **If I take paid Maternity Leave, is the duration of my Maternity Leave less?**

No; you are entitled to 52 weeks of Maternity Leave regardless of whether any of this is paid or not.

9. How long do I receive Statutory Maternity Pay for?

If you are entitled to claim Statutory Maternity Pay, then this is paid for a maximum of 39 weeks.

In the first six weeks of your Maternity Leave you will receive 90% of your average pay and for the remaining 33 weeks of you Statutory Maternity Pay period you are paid £139.58 per week (2016/2017), or 90% of your average earnings if that is lower.

10.Do I have to repay the Statutory Maternity Pay that I have received if I do not return to work?

No; if you do not return to work after your Maternity Leave then you do not have to repay any of the Statutory Maternity Pay that you have received.

ABOUT THE AUTHOR

From the age of 11, and just before starting at High School, Leah knew she wanted to become a solicitor when she 'grew up'!

Leah studied for her GCSEs and then undertook A Level studies in English Literature, History, Psychology and Sociology before moving to Wales and reading for her Bachelor of Laws (LLB) at The University of Glamorgan and going on to complete her Legal Practice Course at Cardiff University.

Throughout Leah's early career, and during her Training Contract, she has dealt with a variety of areas of law including Personal Injury, Dispute Resolution and Litigation, Debt Recovery, Wills and Lasting Powers of Attorney and Possession Claims but has always had a passion for Employment Law and began her legal career training under the supervision of a former Employment Tribunal Judge.

Leah also worked for a short period in the Commercial sector before recently joining Lennons Solicitors in Chesham, in July 2016, as their Employment Law Specialist and Head of the Employment Law Department.

Leah runs a seminar programme holding Employment Law seminars for both employees and employers to keep you up to date with your legal rights and giving you practical advice and welcomes any suggestions for future topics.

Leah can be contacted in any of the following ways:-

Email -   leah.waller@lennonssolicitors.co.uk

Twitter -   @Leah_W_88

LinkedIn -   https://uk.linkedin.com/in/leahwaller88

CPSIA information can be obtained
at www.ICGtesting.com
Printed in the USA
LVOW13s2251310117

522808LV00002B/21/P

9 781911 035053